# ADVENTURES IN COMMUNITY SCIENCE

## WORKBOOK

Designed by Lisa Smith and Jack Chappell
Illustrations by Lily Smith and Karen Acton
All photos by the author unless otherwise noted
Type set in True North/Yonder/Frutiger

ISBN: 978-0-7643-6576-8
Printed in China

Published by Schiffer Kids
An imprint of Schiffer Publishing, Ltd.
4880 Lower Valley Road
Atglen, PA 19310
Phone: (610) 593-1777; Fax: (610) 593-2002
Email: info@schifferbooks.com
Web: www.schiffer-kids.com

For our complete selection of fine books on this and related subjects, please visit our website at www.schifferbooks.com. You may also write for a free catalog.

Schiffer Publishing's titles are available at special discounts for bulk purchases for sales promotions or premiums. Special editions, including personalized covers, corporate imprints, and excerpts, can be created in large quantities for special needs. For more information, contact the publisher.

FSC
www.fsc.org
MIX
Paper from
responsible sources
FSC® C167893

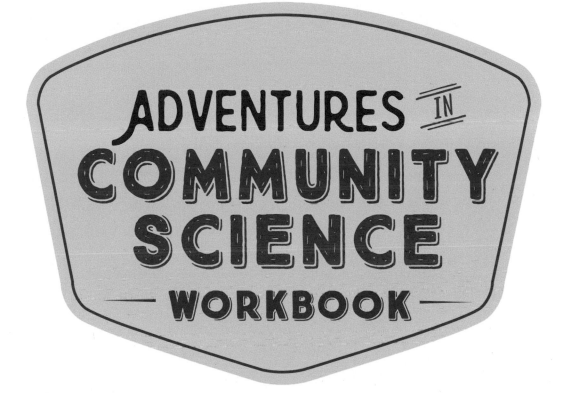

# ADVENTURES IN COMMUNITY SCIENCE WORKBOOK

## 14 INVESTIGATIONS CONNECTED TO ACTUAL COMMUNITY-BASED INITIATIVES

### RON SMITH

ILLUSTRATIONS BY LILY SMITH

AND KAREN ACTON

4880 Lower Valley Road, Atglen, PA 19310

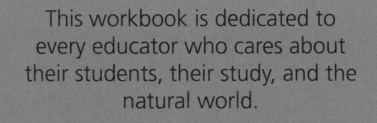

This workbook is dedicated to every educator who cares about their students, their study, and the natural world.

-RON SMITH

# CONTENTS

## WELCOME TO THE ADVENTURES IN COMMUNITY SCIENCE WORKBOOK!

As educators, whether parents or teachers, what do we want for you, our students and children, in education? We want you to be curious. We want you to explore. We want you to ask questions. We want you to care about each other and the Earth. We want you to see connections. We want you to feel that learning is fun. This is true whether we are leading a class of kindergarten students, a summer nature project, or a college course (I have done all three during almost thirty years as an educator). If you don't see the relevance of what you are learning and don't make connections between subjects and don't enjoy your studies and explorations, education becomes merely a process—one more thing to check off from the list of things you have to do in life. Often, when speaking with adults, I have noticed that many of the things they remember from their early years in education were lessons introduced to them by a person who had passion and a unique approach to sharing what they love. This can and should be what we strive to achieve in education.

In the companion book *Adventures in Community Science*, stories of adventure combine with the thrill of discovery and the realization that science can be learned while students contribute to the welfare of the planet. In this supplementary workbook, you have the opportunity to connect the stories and themes from the *Adventures in Community Science* text to investigations that span the subjects of science, math, geography, writing, and art. So whether you choose to participate in one topic or plan for a sequence of lessons covering the entire workbook, you will see the value in the activities found on these pages—and enjoy the excitement that comes from being a community scientist!

In the spirit of conservation, discovery, and sharing, enjoy your adventures!

**RON SMITH**

# "HORSESHOE CRAB RESCUE" INVESTIGATIONS

Horseshoe crabs need your help! Due to the presence of man-made structures such as pilings and seawalls, these ancient creatures are frequently trapped during their annual mating season. Without rescue efforts, many will perish, and the population will continue to decline.

## NATURAL HISTORY RECAP

**What do we know about horseshoe crabs?** Not actually crabs at all, horseshoe crabs are more closely related to spiders and scorpions than crustaceans. Named for the shape of their shell, or carapace, these marine invertebrates migrate into the bays of the East Coast of the United States seeking quiet, sandy beaches to spawn (lay and fertilize their eggs). With a tough exoskeleton and six pairs of legs to feed and crawl, the only time they leave the water is to lay their eggs in the spring and early summer.

During this time, the female digs down into the sand and deposits eggs, which will be fertilized by the males. Not all the tiny green eggs hatch, and those that do not hatch become food for many species in and around the bay ecosystem, including migratory shorebirds. Those that survive will emerge after a few weeks as young horseshoe crabs. In order to grow, they must shed their hard exoskeleton, or molt. Before they reach adult size, which will take around eight years or so, they may molt up to twenty times! Adult crabs will migrate out of the bay in late summer and spend the winter in deeper water offshore, only to return to the bay shore beaches the next spring.

Female (*large*) and male (*small*) horseshoe crabs

**Why are horseshoe crabs in trouble?** For over a hundred years, horseshoe crabs have faced danger directly from humans. Once collected for fertilizer, they are now harvested for bait. Some are taken to labs where their blood is collected because it is used to check medicines for contamination by bacteria. Rising seas are eroding beaches where crabs spawn, and on other beaches, human structures such as seawalls and pilings trap them.

**How can we help?** The efforts of volunteers who flip and rescue horseshoe crabs save tens of thousands of crabs every spring. Though horseshoe crabs have been around much longer than the dinosaurs, all four species of horseshoe crabs are threatened with extinction!

## MALE-TO-FEMALE RATIOS

### LESSON OVERVIEW

The emergence of horseshoe crabs on spawning beaches reveals an interesting fact. The ratio of females to males is not equal. The number of males typically is greater than the number of females. In this activity you will explore the ratio of rescued males and females and compare these values to the ratio of spawning crabs.

### LEARNING OBJECTIVES

1. Examine the horseshoe crabs, males versus females, in a rescue sample.
2. Compare the ratio of male to female from rescue count to the ratio from spawning count.
3. Explore ideas on how different beach conditions will affect the ratio of males to females.

Stranded horseshoe crabs await rescue.

During the spring spawn, researchers have counted the number of males and females to determine the ratio. Typically this ranges from 2:1 to 5:1 (males to females).

Below is a diagram that shows what we might find on one of our rescues. Rubble piles are one of a few different ways in which horseshoe crabs can get trapped when they come up to spawn. These piles are the remains of buildings and other human structures damaged by storms or simply neglected over time. Large crabs in the image are females, and smaller crabs are males.

## TASKS

1. Count the total crabs present and write the ratio of males to females in this sample.
2. How does your ratio compare to what researchers find during spawning activity?
3. What could be a reason for the difference in the ratio you found?
4. Some of the crabs we find have died, and others are alive and active. What do you think will affect whether or not a crab survives being trapped?

MALE

FEMALE

# INVESTIGATION 2

## SPAWNING BEACHES: RESCUE DATA AND HABITAT IMPACT

### LESSON OVERVIEW

Beaches where horseshoe crabs spawn can be affected by various human activities. Homes and development along the beaches, debris and rubble from storms, and erosion along the coastline from rising sea levels all impact the success of spawning along beaches. In this activity you will investigate rescued horseshoe crab abundance and the types of shoreline features that impact them during the spawning season.

### LEARNING OBJECTIVES

1. Read the maps to establish the different features (human or natural) present.
2. Understand how distance is represented on a map, using a map scale.
3. Calculate the percentage of the beach with different feature coverage.
4. Establish the quality of habitat for horseshoe crabs as determined from the map study.
5. Graph crab rescue data from sample sites.

### TASKS

1. Measure the length of each beach (1 cm = 100 m).
   The symbols for beach composition (natural or human materials found on the beach) are shown in the diagram.
2. Calculate the percentage of the beach on the basis of each feature shown above.
   Example: If the total beach is 1 km (10 cm measured) and 4 cm is sand and 6 cm is rubble,
   4 cm sand / 10 cm total beach × 100 = 40% sand
   6 cm rubble / 10 cm total beach × 100 = 60% rubble
3. For each beach, calculate the percentage of horseshoe crabs that are trapped and flipped.
4. Which beach has the best horseshoe crab spawning habitat? Explain.
5. Which beach has the worst horseshoe crab spawning habitat? Explain.

## BEACH MAPS FOR SPAWNING HORSESHOE CRABS

The map on page 13 shows four spawning beaches for horseshoe crabs.
Note: all sites have a history of horseshoe crab spawning.

# "NIGHT LIGHTS" INVESTIGATIONS

Fireflies that light up the night in your backyard need your help! All types of invertebrates are in trouble as a result of habitat loss, pesticide use, and other human threats. Insects and other creature groups provide important services that humans and all species need to survive. Many species are tricky to monitor, so we rely on readily observable species to serve as indicators for the health of our backyards, parks, and other natural places. Cue the fireflies!

## NATURAL HISTORY RECAP

**What do we know about fireflies?** Fireflies, also called lightning bugs, are neither flies nor bugs (bugs are actually a specific group of insects). Instead, they are beetles. The most diverse group of insects, beetles are found everywhere. Cousins to the familiar ladybird beetles (also called ladybugs), fireflies can be found in some of the same habitats. Normally, insect studies require collection. Many different kinds of traps are used, set at day or night, to catch various insect species. It is part of the biology of the firefly that allows us to study them without catching any.

Firefly on a glass window. *Suzanne Tucker / Shutterstock*

More than 150 species of North American firefly occupy habitats that include meadows, forest edges, and fields. Many of these habitat types can be found in your backyard or close by in a park or garden. Though they do not need to be close to large bodies of water, they do need ready access to moisture. As larvae their diet consists of small invertebrates, and as adults they eat various insects (including other fireflies) and plant food such as pollen or nectar. Their diverse diet makes them important, since they control the populations of other invertebrates and pollinate various types of plants.

**Why are fireflies so important?** Though not all fireflies are bioluminescent, most species do display the almost magical flashing that they are known for. It is this part of their biology that makes them so familiar to many kids and adults and makes them useful as biological indicators. Sharing habitats with many other insect species, fireflies can serve as indicators of environmental health. In backyards, gardens, parks, and forests, a thriving firefly population indicates an ecosystem that is likely to be healthy for other creatures. However, low numbers of fireflies, or their absence, in suitable habitat can indicate just the opposite—that something is causing the habitat not to be able to support invertebrates.

**How can we help?** Not only can you create habitat that is firefly friendly in your backyard, school garden, or local park, but you can also monitor their populations during the spring and summer. This will allow you to determine if local habitats are healthy for fireflies and other types of invertebrates—insects, spiders, crustaceans, worms, and snails, among others!

Small meadow patch for firefly habitat

# INVESTIGATION 1

## THE EFFECTS OF LIGHT POLLUTION

### LESSON OVERVIEW

These backyard luminaries entertain and delight children and adults alike. As a sign of appreciation for all the joy they bring, we can go a long way to enhance our gardens and yards to ensure a healthy habitat for these beetles. It is the very same thing that we find fascinating about them that can also be the way to monitor their health.

The study below reveals firefly flash frequency and the effects of light pollution. The values found for each data set represent the number of flashes for ten different days during June and July. For each of the data sets below, the number indicates the number of flashes per minute counted in a 15-by-15-meter (50 × 50 foot) garden.

### LEARNING OBJECTIVES

1. Evaluate the number of flashes from fireflies.
2. Create a column graph to compare firefly data from different gardens.
3. Use firefly biology to explain the outcome of the study.
4. Research and describe other species that use bioluminescence.
5. Design an experiment to test a hypothesis.

| DATA SET 1 | DATA SET 2 | DATA SET 3 | DATA SET 4 |
|------------|------------|------------|------------|
| 112 | 97 | 32 | 7 |
| 120 | 81 | 25 | 4 |
| 153 | 102 | 18 | 8 |
| 144 | 68 | 20 | 5 |
| 134 | 88 | 21 | 6 |
| 129 | 79 | 30 | 10 |
| 156 | 86 | 16 | 5 |
| 138 | 90 | 19 | 4 |
| 122 | 103 | 25 | 6 |
| 163 | 99 | 22 | 7 |

**Data set 1—Dark garden, with adjacent gardens dark as well (no exterior lights on)**

**Data set 2—Dark garden, with outdoor lights on in adjacent gardens**

**Data set 3—Lights on in garden, with adjacent gardens dark**

**Data set 4—Lights on in garden and adjacent gardens**

## TASKS

1. Calculate the mean (average number) of flashes/minute for all data sets.
2. Produce a column graph displaying the average values from the first task (see resources in appendix 2 for help if needed).
3. Write a summary of the findings. What did the researchers find? What does this say about the effects of lights on firefly activity?
4. Think about why fireflies display their flashes. What activities of fireflies could be affected by too much light?
5. Research three other species of nocturnal animals that could be affected by light pollution. Describe what the effects of lights could be on these species.
6. Researchers have established that using red lights can reduce the impact on nocturnal insects and other animals. Design an experiment to test this hypothesis.

# FIREFLY BACKYARD HABITAT - TEMPLATE

# INVESTIGATION 2

## DESIGNING A FIREFLY HABITAT

### LESSON OVERVIEW

Every creature has basic needs in its habitat. Human structures and activities can affect species by taking away an important feature or resource in their habitat. In this activity you will design a backyard garden to support fireflies. You will be provided various garden features and basic guidelines on what to include in your plan to support fireflies.

### LEARNING OBJECTIVES

1. Identify the habitat needs of a firefly.
2. Collaborate with a team to design a backyard habitat to support fireflies.
3. Present your backyard habitat design to your learning community.

### TASKS

1. Cut out the habitat features from the template provided, or download them from www.schiffer-kids.com/communityscience. A key to identify the features is available on page 22.

2. Measure the total area of the backyard template provided. Multiply one side by the other and establish your area in square inches or centimeters.

3. Plan your ideal backyard firefly habitat. **You must use at least one of each of the ten features and cannot use any more than five of the same feature in your design.** Plan your garden but do not attach the features to your backyard template until you (or your group) settle on the layout.

4. Provide a written description of your habitat design and layout. Describe why you used the features you included and why you placed them where you did.

## GARDEN HABITAT DESIGN

**Use the backyard garden template and the various habitat features provided to plan your area.
You can also visit www.schiffer-kids.com/communityscience for downloadable sheets for this activity.**

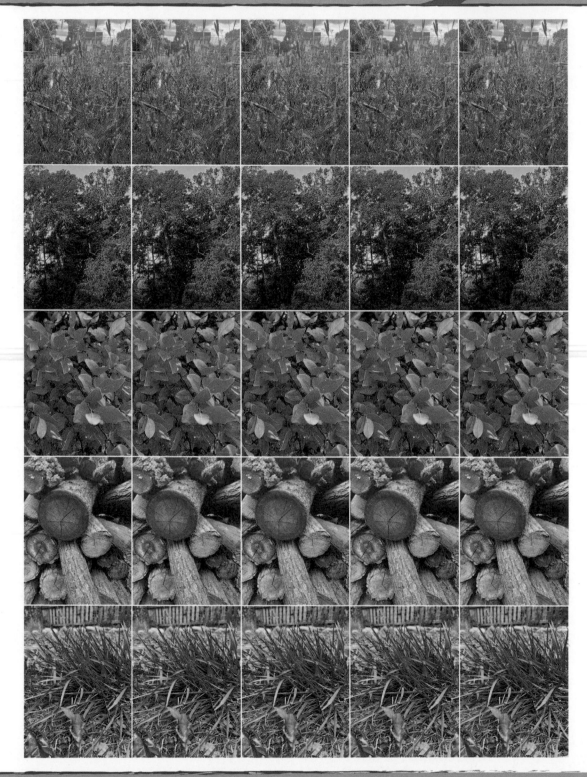

# FIREFLY BACKYARD HABITAT FEATURES

# KEY-FIREFLY BACKYARD HABITAT FEATURES

MEADOW

TREES

SHRUBS

WOODPILE

GRASS

LEAF LITTER

SOIL

WATER FEATURE

BRICK OR STONE WALK

FENCE

# "FINDING FROGS" INVESTIGATIONS

As one of the most threatened groups of animals, frogs and toads need your help. Climate-driven changes to their wetland habitats, new roads that are dividing their breeding grounds, and pesticide runoff from nearby farms and gardens all threaten amphibians. It is up to us to collect the needed data to find out how our amphibian friends are doing and to complete an ecological checkup of their native habitats.

## NATURAL HISTORY RECAP

**What do we know about amphibians?** Frogs and toads are amphibians, the group of mostly small, four-legged, cold-blooded vertebrates that also includes salamanders. Different from reptiles, amphibians lay their eggs in water and do not have scales. Their skin is very permeable—great for getting oxygen but bad when it comes to air and water pollution. Most amphibians undergo metamorphosis, a dramatic change in body form and function as they develop from egg to larva to adult.

Handfuls of frogs on survey night in the Pine Barrens

The vast majority of frogs and toads lay their eggs in aquatic habitats. The diversity of these freshwater habitats can be surprising—from naturally acidic water bodies to temporary pools (sometimes called vernal pools) that hold water for only part of the year. Breeding in these types of habitats reduces the threat from predators, since fish are usually not found in temporary aquatic habitats. Some species will actually breed in watery habitats created by people (such as drainage basins or rain gardens)!

While they are developing within their eggs, frogs and toads get all they need from the yolk and the movement of oxygen across the eggs, which must be kept moist. Hatching can take anywhere from a few days to a few weeks. Emerging as tadpoles with tails and gills, they will remain completely aquatic during this stage of their life. Their diet is omnivorous (they may eat plant or animal matter) while in the tadpole stage. Developing into adults within weeks to months, they will now be able to emerge on land. As adults they will be almost exclusively carnivorous and now breath with lungs, though many can also obtain oxygen across their skin. Many frogs will stay fairly close to aquatic habitats, but many toads will move surprisingly far from water.

Generally speaking, frogs are more tied to aquatic habitats throughout their lives when compared with toads. However, both breed in water, with toads typically laying a string of eggs, while many frogs lay an egg cluster. Most frogs have smoother, moister skin when compared with the drier, bumpier skin of toads. There are exceptions to these comparisons, but these characteristics are helpful for identifying the basic differences.

**Why are amphibians in danger?** Amphibians have life stages that require healthy habitats in both aquatic and terrestrial environments. As such they are especially vulnerable to human activities that might affect one or both of these ecosystems. In addition, their skin is very permeable to pollutants, so pesticides and other chemicals can harm them more so than other species. Some species migrate to breeding locations. Although they may move only short distances, roads and other human features can separate them from needed habitat and can put them at risk from vehicles or other threats. Introduced species in aquatic habitats can outcompete frogs and toads for food, or the frogs themselves might be the food for invasive predators. As if these threats were not enough, scientists have identified a fungus that has spread across much of the planet and is causing harm to frog populations.

**How can we help?** We often try to identify the cause for amphibian declines in various locations. The problem is that there are so many threats in so many locations. This is why people around the world must work together to protect frogs and toads and other amphibians! By studying frogs and toads and surveying their habitats, details can be shared with conservation groups that will use the data to protect the identified species.

# INVESTIGATION 1

## YOUR FROG INVENTORY

### LESSON OVERVIEW

The frog and toad communities across the country vary by habitat and climate. In this study you will list the species found in your state or region and describe the key aspects of natural history and conservation for each. As part of your study, you will review the identification features of each species as well as their call.

### LEARNING OBJECTIVES

1. Identify the frogs and toads found in your area.
2. Research the natural history of each species (life cycle, habitat, reproduction, conservation status, etc.).
3. Learn the key identification features of each species, including its call.
4. Create a field guide of the species in your area, for display and education.

Toadlet takes first hop on land.

## TASKS

1. Access the USGS Frog Quiz website here: https://www.pwrc.usgs.gov/frogquiz
2. Select "Public Quiz."
3. Enter your state in the drop-down menu on the main page. If your state is not active on the USGS website, use a nearby state to find the same or similar amphibian community.
4. Write down the species from your state's list.
5. Using the list of frogs and toads for your area, either from the menu or from natural history resources in your region/state, enter the species one at a time in the USGS "Frog Call Lookup" located in the link at the bottom of the menu.
6. Listen to the call of each species.
7. Describe the call on the field guide worksheet. Imagine you want a friend to be able to identify the species without seeing it.
8. Look up the habitat for each species and record.
9. Look up the conservation status of each species and enter in your field guide worksheet.
10. Rank the species from your list in order of priority for a community science effort to monitor in your state or region.
11. When you are ready to take the quiz, click on the "Take Quiz" button for your state or region. Quiz yourself or your partner(s).

Use the Community Science Data Sheet template in appendix A or download sheets from www.schiffer-kids.com/communityscience to create your field guide and take notes on each species.

Under Project Name, record the species name.

Under Description, record the species and habitat descriptions.

Under Data/Calculations, record the call description.

Under Notes and Sketches, record the conservation status and community science priority ranking.

# INVESTIGATION 2

## PLANNING A FROG-AND-TOAD STUDY

### LESSON OVERVIEW

In this investigation you are in charge of planning a Massachusetts frog-and-toad-breeding survey. The goal is to plan two weeks of study during a period of the year when your study team will be able to collect data on breeding and tadpole development for the maximum number of species. Week 1 has a focus on breeding activity. The second week is to be focused on tadpole abundance. The two weeks can be separate or together during the spring and summer.

Your job is to chart the breeding times and tadpole life stage time for each species on the amphibian activity calendar provided.

### LEARNING OBJECTIVES

1. Collect breeding and tadpole data on frog and toad species from a specific region.
2. Organize data collected into a calendar data table.
3. Discuss with your learning group the options for a breeding and tadpole survey.
4. Recommend two weeks for conducting a breeding and tadpole study on the species listed. Present your findings and recommendation.

The information needed for each species is found in the table below.

| SPECIES | BREEDING SEASON | DAYS TO HATCH | DAYS AS TADPOLE |
|---|---|---|---|
| American bullfrog | late May through July | 5–20 | *about 2 years |
| American toad | early April through July | 3–12 | 35–70 |
| eastern spadefoot toad | April through May | 5–15 | 16–20 |
| Fowler's toad | mid-May through mid-August | 7 | 40–60 |
| gray treefrog | early May through July | 4–5 | 50–60 |
| green frog | April through August | 3–6 | *1–2 years |
| northern leopard frog | March through May | 14–21 | 60–90 |
| pickerel frog | March through May | 11–21 | 80–100 |
| spring peeper | early March through June | 6–12 | 9–100 |
| wood frog | March through July | 10–30 | 40–100 |

Build your amphibian calendar from the template below.

| Species Breeding | MARCH WK 1 | WK 2 | WK 3 | WK 4 | APRIL WK 1 | WK 2 | WK 3 | WK 4 | MAY WK 1 | WK 2 | WK 3 | WK 4 | JUNE WK 1 | WK 2 | WK 3 | WK 4 | JULY WK 1 | WK 2 | WK 3 | WK 4 | AUGUST WK 1 | WK 2 | WK 3 | WK 4 |
|---|---|---|---|---|---|---|---|---|---|---|---|---|---|---|---|---|---|---|---|---|---|---|---|---|
| American bullfrog | | | | | | | | | | | | | | | | | | | | | | | | |
| American toad | | | | | | | | | | | | | | | | | | | | | | | | |
| eastern spadefoot toad | | | | | | | | | | | | | | | | | | | | | | | | |
| Fowler's toad | | | | | | | | | | | | | | | | | | | | | | | | |
| gray tree frog | | | | | | | | | | | | | | | | | | | | | | | | |
| green frog | | | | | | | | | | | | | | | | | | | | | | | | |
| northern leopard frog | | | | | | | | | | | | | | | | | | | | | | | | |
| pickerel frog | | | | | | | | | | | | | | | | | | | | | | | | |
| spring peeper | | | | | | | | | | | | | | | | | | | | | | | | |
| wood frog | | | | | | | | | | | | | | | | | | | | | | | | |

## TASKS

1. For each of the species listed in the study, place an "X" in the boxes where breeding is likely to occur and an "O" in the boxes when tadpoles are likely to be present.
2. After the table is filled in, select one week for maximum species diversity during the breeding season.
3. Select a second week for maximum diversity of tadpole activity.
4. Provide a summary of your selection process and survey timing recommendation.
5. Do you have recommendations or ideas for further study for this regional frog and toad survey? Describe.

**RESOURCES:**

www.massherpatlas.org/amphibians_reptiles/

https://www.massaudubon.org/learn/nature-wildlife/reptiles-amphibians/frogs/frog-species-in-massachusetts

# "MYSTERY MUSSEL" INVESTIGATIONS

Did you know that 70% of all freshwater mussels in North America are threatened with extinction? Perhaps the most endangered group of animals you have never heard of, freshwater mussels are very accessible to those who seek them out. Because they live in freshwater habitats that flow across landscapes, we can predict the health of their populations and communities on the basis of the land use around their watery homes.

## NATURAL HISTORY RECAP

**What do we know about freshwater mussels?** Not as well known as their edible marine cousins, freshwater mussels are a diverse group of bivalve mollusks that live embedded in the sand, silt, mud, and pebble bottoms of streams and rivers around the world. They vary in size from the tiny littlewing pearly mussel to the giant Chinese pond mussel. Regardless of size or shape, every mussel has two shells held together by a strong muscle (mussels have muscles!). Moving along the bottom, a mussel will partially bury itself in the river bottom by using an extendable body part called the foot. Once in place, the mussel can bring in water to feed on small bits of organic matter and tiny organisms using a tubelike siphon. The filtered water is then released from another siphon. Oxygen is also obtained in this way.

As mussels filter the water that flows past, they help clean the stream or river of excess particles, algae, and organic matter, which could otherwise increase to unhealthy levels. Mussel larvae and adults are also part of freshwater food webs, with many species of aquatic animals relying on them for food (as well as terrestrial species that visit the water searching for a meal).

Even dead mussels can be important for freshwater habitats. The shells of mussels can accumulate and create a firm surface upon which other species can live. The diversity of habitats in a healthy stream or river is made possible by mussels!

**Why are freshwater mussels in danger?** The land that drains into a body of water is called a watershed. Water flowing across, near, and through forests, farms, cities, and streets can lead to nutrients, sediment, and many other potential pollutants ending up in a stream or river. The filter-feeding habits of mussels can result in the accumulation of toxic chemicals in their bodies. Where sediment levels are high, their habitat— and even the mussels themselves—can be covered over. As streams and rivers are dammed and diverted, changes in water flow can change their habitat. The fish species that are needed for their successful reproduction can be affected similarly by changes in water quality and flow, and so even if mussels hang on in a habitat, without their fish partners, successful reproduction can be affected. Other threats include invasive species, which may outcompete the mussels for food and habitat, and climate change, which can alter water levels or dry out shallow streams.

Freshwater mussels to be measured

**How can we help?** By teaming up with other intrepid investigators to document the condition of your local stream or river and by identifying and measuring the mussels in your area, you can determine the health of the habitat. Many mussels species are imperiled and are protected by law, so your data can help local or regional conservation efforts.

# INVESTIGATION 1

## MUSSEL MAPPING

### LESSON OVERVIEW

The diversity of freshwater mussels is greater in North America than anywhere else in the world. Over 250 species are found across the continent, and certain regions—deemed mussel hotspots—can have over one hundred species within a single large watershed. Mussels face many challenges, including changing water levels, pollution, invasive species, and dams along rivers and streams.

If you want to understand the effects of human activities on freshwater mussels, you have to know the human activities and the landscape features in your watershed. Is healthy forest present? Are there farms nearby? Do roads and other impervious surfaces drain into a given stream? In this investigation you will examine a watershed map that shows human and natural features and the connectivity of streams and rivers. Four mussel study sites are found on the map at different locations. Your job will be to match mussel diversity data with the corresponding location on the map. More species will be present where healthy habitat can be found.

## LEARNING OBJECTIVES

1. Read a watershed map and describe the human and natural features.
2. Describe how different human impacts can affect freshwater mussels.
3. Connect mussel diversity with the health of the habitat.

## PART 1: HUMAN IMPACTS ON MUSSELS
## TASKS

1. For each of the following human impacts, describe how mussel survival is threatened (you may need to use online resources for this task):
    (A) agricultural runoff (fertilizers, pesticides, and sediment)
    (B) dams (blocking the flow of the river or stream)
    (C) invasive aquatic species (species that have been introduced to freshwater habitats, whose populations grow largely unchecked)
    (D) climate change (changes in precipitation and temperature patterns)

## PART 2: MUSSEL MAPS
## TASKS

2. Describe the impacts of each landscape type from the mussel map on page 31.
3. Match the mussel communities (described in the box on page 31) with the sample locations (A, B, C, and D) on the map. Explain your reasoning.
4. Present your findings to the other learning groups. Did all groups match the same data sets with study sites? Explain why or why not.

This map shows the interconnected streams and rivers of a watershed and the land use throughout the region. Each lettered site references a location where mussel diversity was sampled.

The list below provides the species richness (the number of different species) found within the watershed at a designated site.

Community 1:  1 species of mussel

Community 2:  2 species of mussels

Community 3:  5 species of mussels

Community 4:  8 species of mussels

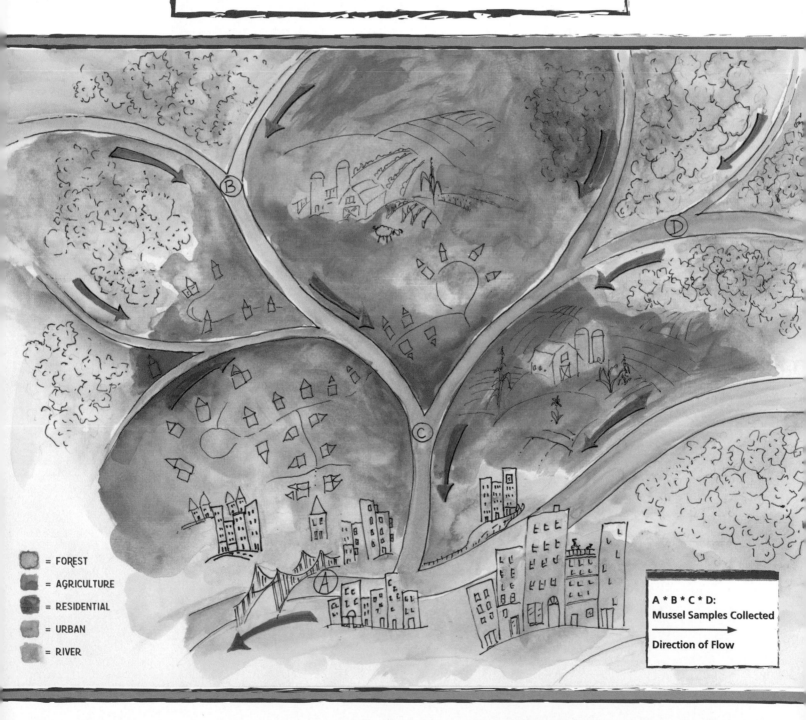

= FOREST

= AGRICULTURE

= RESIDENTIAL

= URBAN

= RIVER

A * B * C * D:
Mussel Samples Collected

→ Direction of Flow

# INVESTIGATION 2

## HOW TO IDENTIFY A FRESHWATER MUSSEL

### LESSON OVERVIEW

The following samples of freshwater mussels were collected at field sites throughout the Delaware River watershed. The stream or river bottom habitat is provided for each specimen. For this activity you will be using the features of each mussel, a ruler, and the habitat description for each specimen to identify and report on the species found within the Delaware River watershed.

### LEARNING OBJECTIVES

1. Identify the mussel species present in the Delaware River watershed.
2. Determine the length and width of mussel specimens and confirm that the size matches your identification from the field guide.
3. Match habitat descriptions with field guide information to confirm mussel identifications.

### TASKS

1. Using the online mussel field guide, look up the four unknown specimens provided.
2. Use a ruler to measure the length and width of the unknown specimens.
3. Match the stream/river habitat where each specimen was found with the information in the field guides.
4. Confirm the identification of the four freshwater mussels collected from the watershed.

### DESCRIPTION FOR EACH MYSTERY MUSSEL (LISTED FROM TOP TO BOTTOM):

MM-01: Found in a slow-moving stream in Pennsylvania. Stream bottom was sandy with some small gravel.

MM-02: Found in a small, slow-moving river in an urban park in New Jersey. River bottom was mostly mud, with some silt and sand.

MM-03: Found in a small, slow-moving stream in Delaware. Stream bottom was mostly sand.

MM-04: Found in a small, slow-moving stream in Pennsylvania. Stream bottom was variable, with gravel, sand, and some cobbles.

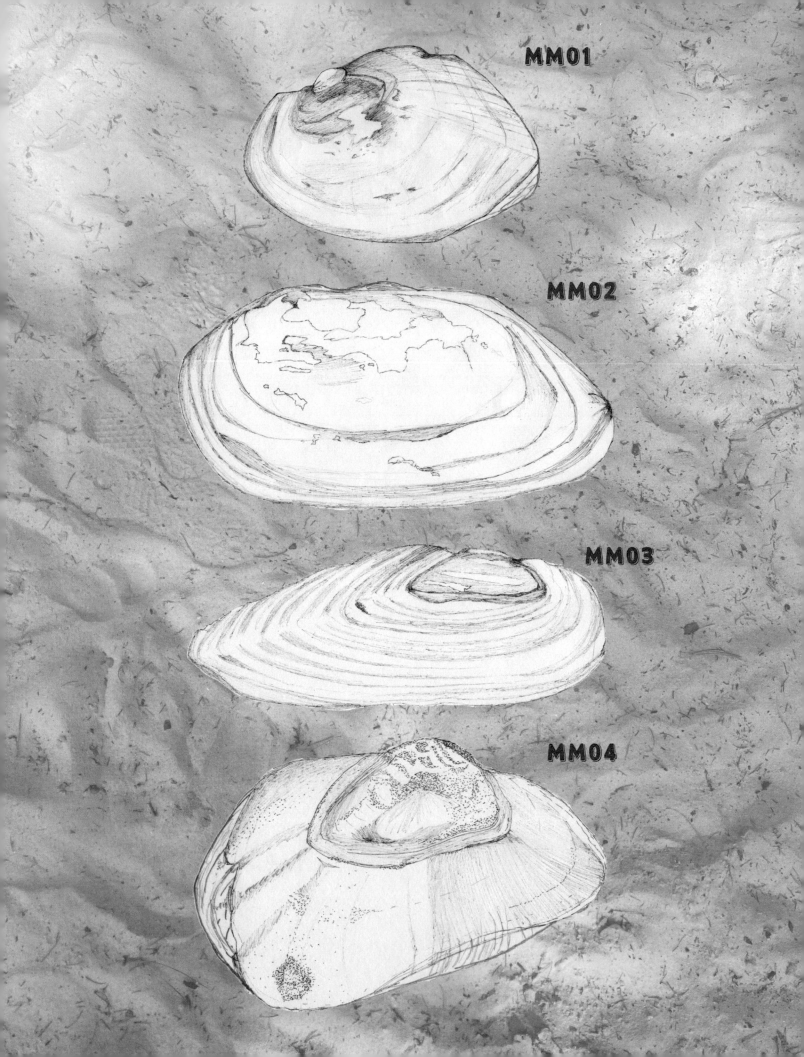

MM01

MM02

MM03

MM04

A community scientist holds a freshwater mussel.

# "THE LANTERNFLY HAS LANDED" INVESTIGATIONS

Lanternflies are well established in four states and have been spotted (no pun intended) in several other states. Though they are poor fliers, they can move considerable distances, and egg masses, larvae, and adults travel readily by human activities. Hitching rides on cars, trailers, and anything else that humans move around, lanternflies can move many miles in a surprisingly short period of time.

## NATURAL HISTORY RECAP

**What do we know about spotted lanternflies?** Native to China, India, and other countries in Asia, the spotted lanternfly is not a fly, as its name might suggest, and not a moth, as its appearance might suggest, but instead a plant hopper, which belongs to a group of insects called "true bugs" or Hemiptera. Meaning "half winged," all members of the Hemiptera have antennae that are divided into small segments, and wings that are thicker at the base and overlap at their tips. With about 80,000 different species, the group is very diverse, but all species, including the spotted lanternfly, have piercing or sucking mouthparts.

Arriving in Pennsylvania in 2012 on a shipment of landscape stone, the first outbreak of lanternflies was described two years later. Lanternflies undergo incomplete metamorphosis (unlike the more familiar life cycle of the butterfly, which uses complete metamorphosis). The eggs hatch from gray, puttylike deposits on trees and other surfaces in May and June. Over the next several weeks the larvae undergo four stages called instars. The first stages reveal a small black bug with white spots, and right before developing into adults the final instar shows black and red with white spots. The adults, about an inch long, have the namesake spots, and when the wings open, flashes of red color are seen with black-and-white coloration. Males and females have yellow abdomens, but females also have red tips at the end of the abdomen. Mating occurs around August, and egg laying can take place through November. Freezing temperatures will kill the adults as fall approaches winter.

Lanternfly nymphs in spring

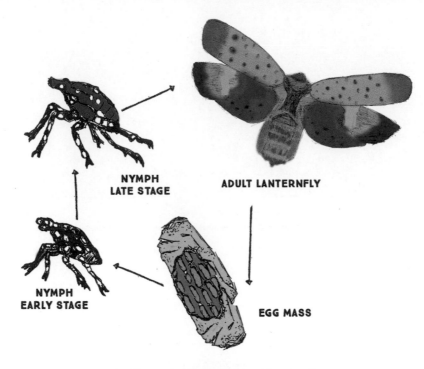

**NYMPH LATE STAGE**

**ADULT LANTERNFLY**

**NYMPH EARLY STAGE**

**EGG MASS**

▲ Life cycle of the spotted lanternfly
▼ Ailanthus: a preferred tree of the spotted lanternfly

**Why are these beautiful insects so harmful?** In North America, lanternflies feed on ailanthus, or tree of heaven, as a preferred food source. Piercing the surface of its host plant, the lanternfly sucks the sap. Other favorite trees for the lanternflies include black walnut, maples, tulip poplar, and black cherry. Agricultural crops affected by feeding lanternflies include grapes, peaches, apples, and hops. Damage to trees and crops can be significant, since the plants are left weaker and less protected from other insects and disease. The insects excrete "honeydew" as they feed, and this sugary material can result in the growth of sooty molds, which makes crops unsuitable for sale.

**What can we do to help?** The battle to halt their movements and reduce damage where they exist is coordinated by state agriculture agencies and county and municipal staff, and research assistance is provided by universities. Campaigns to minimize the movement of eggs and adults across state and county boundaries are underway, and various trapping methods have been used to catch larvae and adults. Residents are encouraged to scrape egg masses from trees and other surfaces, and the removal of host trees and plants can limit their population. As more is learned about their activity and movement, communities are hoping to find greater success with their control. No doubt new methods and data will bring about even more strategies as we work to keep these invading insects in check.

Lanternfly trap

# INVESTIGATION 1

## LANTERNFLY NEIGHBORHOOD INVENTORY

### LESSON OVERVIEW

Invasive species cause problems for humans and ecosystems. Their abundance and distribution (how many there are and where they are found) can determine how much damage can be caused in a region. To determine their potential effects in an area, we must collect data on their abundance and distribution. In this study you will examine a data set collected in a suburban neighborhood and determine the preferred host plant for lanternflies and their abundance. Lanternfly data and conservation work can be assigned to a community science group by block. You will be provided with two neighborhood street blocks (see pages 40 and 41). Tree species are to be identified by leaf illustrations, and you will count the total number of lanternflies from each tree and the total number of lanternflies for each block. The average number of species per tree will be determined.

### LEARNING OBJECTIVES

1. Identify tree species from leaf illustrations.
2. Determine the total number of trees of each species and compare the data for two neighborhood blocks.
3. Calculate the average number of lanternflies per tree species.
4. Create pie and column graphs to display your data.
5. Compare two study sites (neighborhood blocks) affected by lanternflies.
6. Make recommendations for future tree plantings on the basis of the data you analyzed.

### TASKS

1. Using the maps on pages 40 and 41, count how many of each tree species are present and the total number of trees (each leaf = one tree).
2. Determine the total number of lanternflies for each block.
3. For each block, identify how many lanternflies are found on each tree species (add the number of lanternflies for individual trees of the same species).
4. Create a pie graph that shows the number of each tree species per block (make two graphs).
5. Create a column graph of average number of lanternflies per tree species (include both blocks in one graph).
6. Compare the two blocks in terms of trees and lanternfly number. What is the "big picture"?
7. If this town is planning for new tree plantings, what advice would you give them?

# INVESTIGATION 2

## LIMIT THE LEAP

### LESSON OVERVIEW

Spotted lanternflies have been on the East Coast of the US for about ten years. In a short period of time they have spread to several states, and they have the potential to keep spreading. In this study, you will determine from lanternfly distribution maps how far they have moved since first arriving and where they could potentially spread. You will describe ways in which communities can limit the spread of this pesky plant hopper.

### LEARNING OBJECTIVES

1. Describe the lanternfly biology and life stages and how life stages affect their distribution.
2. Calculate the movement of lanternflies over a period of four years.
3. Evaluate and describe ways to limit the movement of lanternflies and capture individuals from existing areas.

### TASKS

1. Examine the lanternfly infestation maps on pages 42 and 43. The four maps show the presence of lanternfly infestation from 2019 to 2022. How many states have infestations each year? What are the states?
2. Use the scale bar from the map, which indicates distance on the maps per centimeter, to determine the distance the lanternflies have traveled compared with the center of the 2019 infestation (measure from the center of the 2019 infestation to the farthest geographic distance for each year—2019, 2020, 2021, 2022). Indicate directions (N, S, E, W), state, and distance in miles and kilometers.
3. What could explain why lanternfly distribution is not continuous? In other words, why are the locations where lanternfly infestations are found not connected to the larger areas of their distribution?
4. Describe the different ways in which lanternflies can be captured in the regions where they are found. What are the most important things for everyone living in these regions to do, or not do, in order to stop the spread of lanternflies?

## RESOURCE:

**Information on traps and community education can be found here: https://extension.psu.edu/spotted-lanternfly.**

# BLOCK 1
# LANTERNFLY SHADE TREE COMMUNITY STUDY

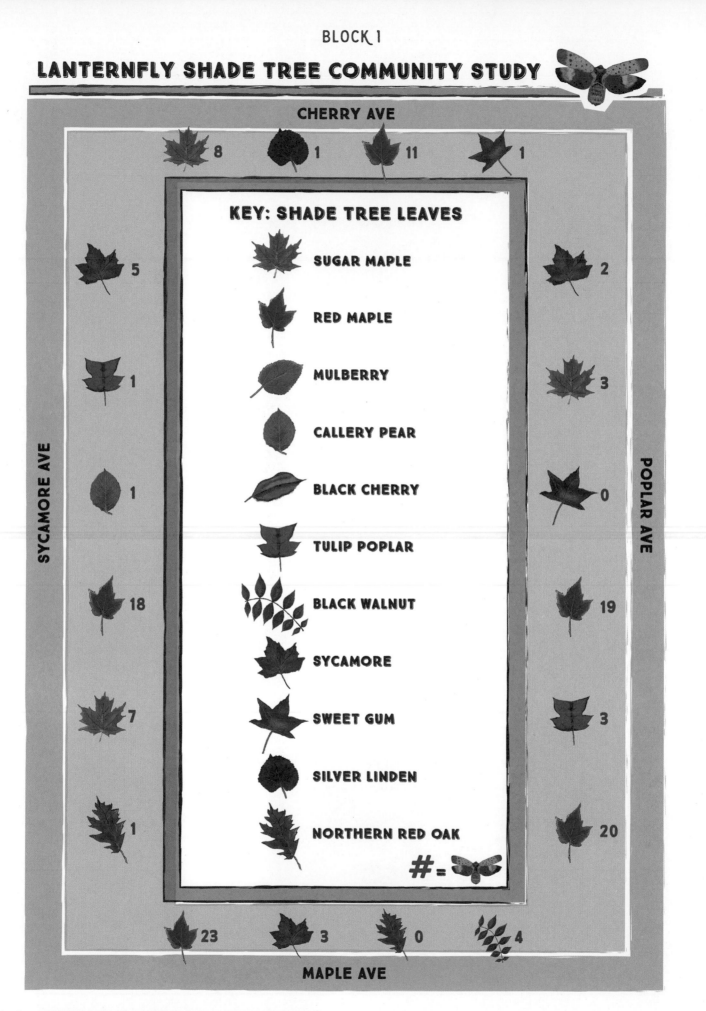

**CHERRY AVE**

8    1    11    1

## KEY: SHADE TREE LEAVES

SUGAR MAPLE

RED MAPLE

MULBERRY

CALLERY PEAR

BLACK CHERRY

TULIP POPLAR

BLACK WALNUT

SYCAMORE

SWEET GUM

SILVER LINDEN

NORTHERN RED OAK

# = 🦋

**SYCAMORE AVE**

5

1

1

18

7

1

**POPLAR AVE**

2

3

0

19

3

20

**MAPLE AVE**

23    3    0    4

# LANTERNFLY SHADE TREE COMMUNITY STUDY

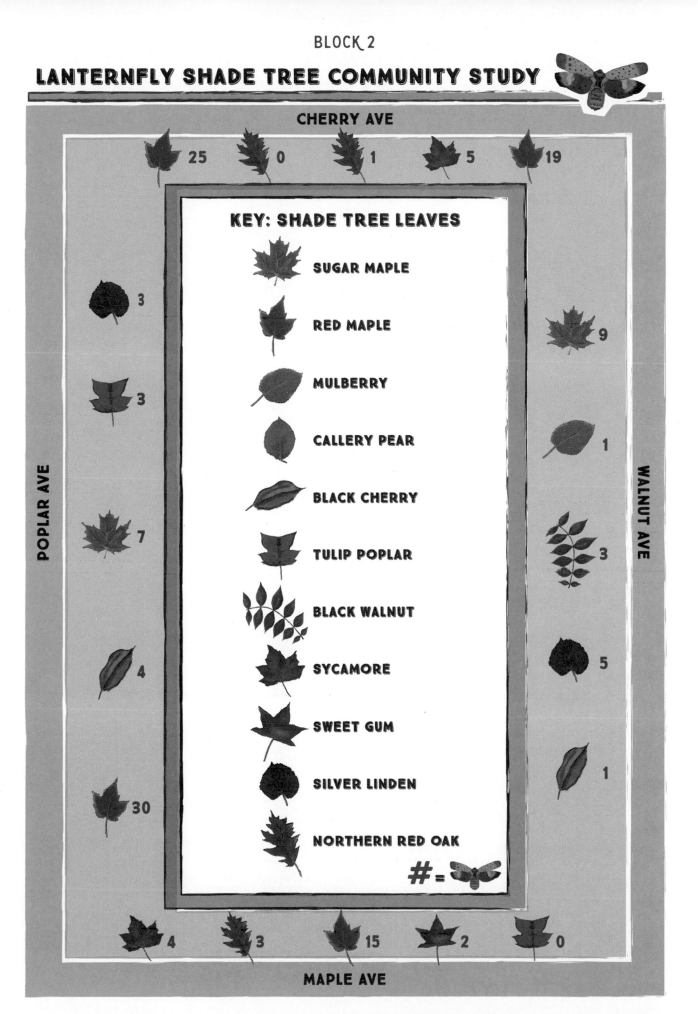

CHERRY AVE

25    0    1    5    19

## KEY: SHADE TREE LEAVES

SUGAR MAPLE

RED MAPLE

MULBERRY

CALLERY PEAR

BLACK CHERRY

TULIP POPLAR

BLACK WALNUT

SYCAMORE

SWEET GUM

SILVER LINDEN

NORTHERN RED OAK

# =

POPLAR AVE

3

3

7

4

30

WALNUT AVE

9

1

3

5

1

MAPLE AVE

4    3    15    2    0

# LANTERNFLY INFESTATION

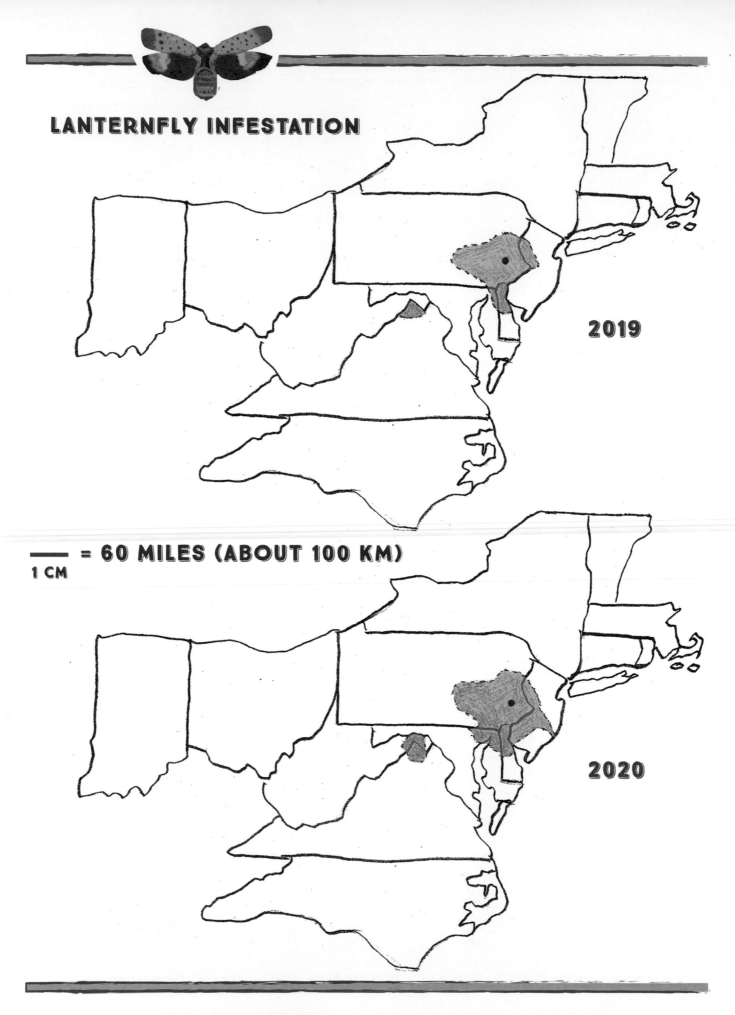

**2019**

**━━━━━** = 60 MILES (ABOUT 100 KM)
1 CM

**2020**

# LANTERNFLY INFESTATION

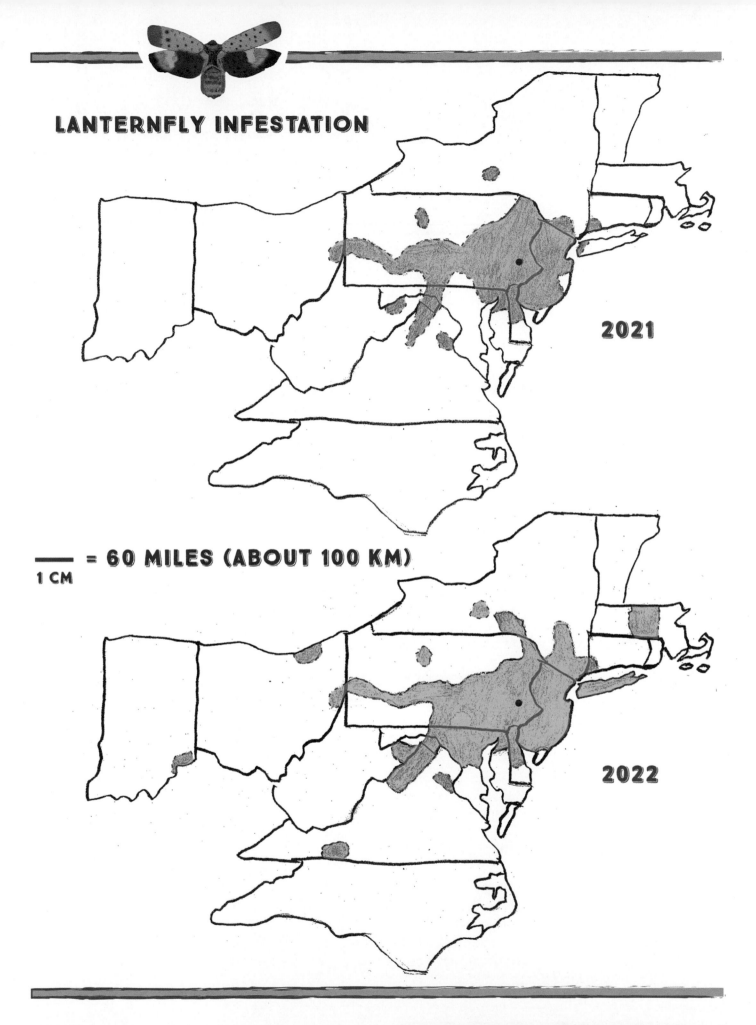

2021

—— = 60 MILES (ABOUT 100 KM)

1 CM

2022

# "THE GREAT SHOREBIRD MIGRATION" INVESTIGATIONS

Summer means migration for various species of shorebirds heading south from their northern breeding grounds in Canada. Along the way they will touch down on various coastal beaches as they head for the gulf shores, while others will travel as far south as the tip of South America. With a little bit of study and practice, we can learn to identify and count these birds; document which species are stopping by on our local beaches, lakeshores, and fields; and estimate their abundance.

## NATURAL HISTORY RECAP

**What do we know about these feathered friends?** Not all birds at the shore are shorebirds, and not all shorebirds are found at the shore. This is a statement that offers an important point about monitoring shorebirds. The group of birds referred to as shorebirds includes over two hundred species worldwide, and about fifty species breed in North America and are typically highly migratory. They have long legs for their body size and have bills that are designed for picking and probing for food items, usually invertebrates. Though many species are found in coastal habitats—marshes, beaches, and mudflats—some do occur along riverbanks and lakeshores and in fields. These birds vary in size from less than 6 inches (such as the least sandpiper) to over 20 inches (such as the long-billed curlew), and size can be useful in identifying similar-looking species.

Migration may be the most incredible part of a shorebird's life. Some individuals can migrate thousands of miles per year and can live as long as twenty years or more. During the longer legs of migration, a shorebird can lose about 50% of its body weight in only a matter of days or weeks. Just as amazing is that some birds can double their body weight within less than three weeks as they gorge on food to prepare for the next part of their journey. This extreme weight loss and gain is part of a fascinating life history that depends heavily on healthy habitats with access to food.

**Why are they in danger?** Shorebirds require healthy habitats at their breeding grounds, wintering grounds, and often multiple stopover sites in between. Being highly migratory automatically makes a species prone to population declines. With climate changing in the Arctic tundra and coastal habitats, oil spills always being a threat along the coast, the need to share habitat with humans at most stopover sites, and the persistence of hunting pressure in some countries, it will come as no surprise that about 75% of shorebird species are in decline, and some are critically endangered.

**How can we help?** With shorebird species widely distributed during all parts of their migration and with so many threats to their survival, the need to monitor these creatures is critical. No matter where you live, it is likely that shorebirds can be found somewhere nearby during some season of the year. Community scientists across the globe are "adopting" locations to keep a careful eye out for an occasional visitor or predictable gatherings of tens of thousands of birds of various species. Join ranks with the scientists who, like you, care about these long-distance migrants!

Red knots drop in for a snack.

# INVESTIGATION 1

## MEET THE SHOREBIRDS: DIVERSITY AND ADAPTATIONS

### LESSON OVERVIEW

Shorebirds have adaptations that make them not only suited to a specific habitat, but also so that they can live alongside other shorebirds that are eating similar food items. In this investigation you will describe key features of shorebirds and identify how these features make them well adapted to the environment in which they are found.

### LEARNING OBJECTIVES

1. Identify key adaptations for shorebirds.
2. Describe how birds that eat similar food items can be found on the same beach but not outcompete one another for food.
3. Match food species (prey) from a beach habitat with shorebird species and describe how specific birds are adapted to specific food items.

The following shorebirds are species that have been observed along the beach at a Mid-Atlantic stopover site:

American oystercatcher
whimbrel
short-billed dowitcher
red knot
ruddy turnstone
sanderling
piping plover

G

F

E

## RESOURCE:

**To access the description of each of the birds listed and for additional information about these shorebirds, visit:**
https://www.allaboutbirds.org/news/

## TASKS

1. Label each shorebird with the correct name from the list. Describe the key differences in the species shown.
2. Offer an idea of how these species are adapted to finding different food items on a beach.

The beach cross sections shown below include invertebrates present that serve as food items for the bird species above.

3. Match each bird species with the invertebrates that they are likely to eat—use key features and your response in task 2 to help you match the prey item with the shorebird species.

# INVESTIGATION 2

## PROTECTING SHOREBIRDS AT STOPOVER SITES

### LESSON OVERVIEW

For migratory birds, we often focus our conservation efforts on the places where they breed or overwinter. But on migration there are also stopover sites that—although they may offer habitat and food only for short periods—are still very important for the survival of these species.

On many beaches, shorebirds can be affected by human activity. The presence of people, pets, and vehicles can scare birds away or keep them from their food sources (or both). In this activity you will determine which human activities affect which bird species, and make recommendations for visitors to our coastlines to take the steps necessary to keep shorebirds safe and ensure they have a healthy habitat to rest and feed on their migration.

### LEARNING OBJECTIVES

1. Identify which human activities on a beach have the greatest impact on shorebirds. Explain your answer on the basis of the data.
2. Document abundance (number of individuals) and richness (number of different species) of shorebirds for five beach sections at a migratory stopover site.
3. Identify bird species that are most affected by human activities.
4. Identify key conservation strategies for shorebirds on a beach.

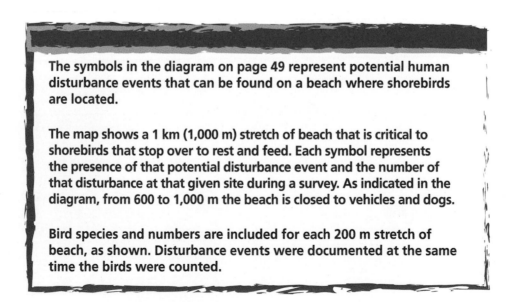

The symbols in the diagram on page 49 represent potential human disturbance events that can be found on a beach where shorebirds are located.

The map shows a 1 km (1,000 m) stretch of beach that is critical to shorebirds that stop over to rest and feed. Each symbol represents the presence of that potential disturbance event and the number of that disturbance at that given site during a survey. As indicated in the diagram, from 600 to 1,000 m the beach is closed to vehicles and dogs.

Bird species and numbers are included for each 200 m stretch of beach, as shown. Disturbance events were documented at the same time the birds were counted.

## TASKS

1. From the list of human activities included in the diagram, predict which would result in the greatest potential disturbance to shorebirds. Rank from most problematic to least. Explain your ranking.

2. Describe the effect of the human activities on each 200 m beach segment on the shorebirds—consider both how many different species and how many total birds are observed.

3. Which species seem most affected by human disturbance? Which human activities seem to cause the greatest disturbance? How does this compare to your predictions in task 1?

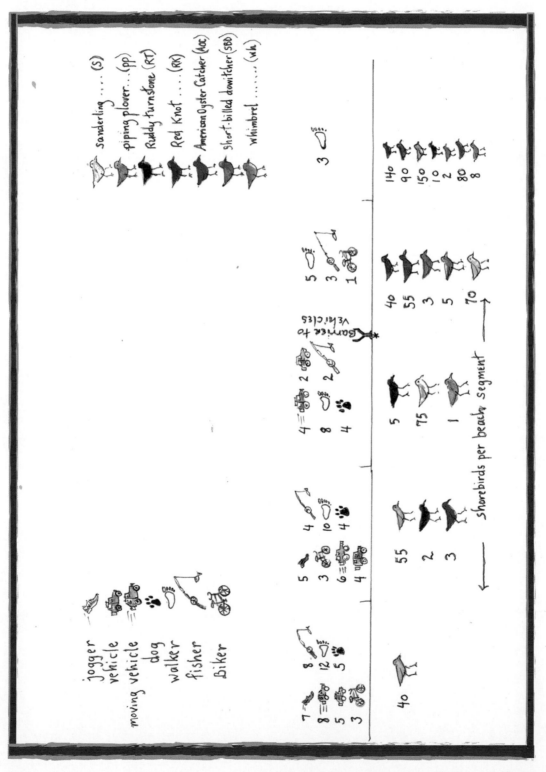

# "SOS—SAVE OUR SPIDERS" INVESTIGATIONS

Though often unwelcomed within our homes, spiders thrive under furniture and in basements, crawl spaces, attics, barns, cabinets, and house plants. Both in the wild and around humans, spiders perform an important service—to keep insect and other invertebrate populations in check. They will reduce aphid populations, which can destroy crops; reduce mosquitoes, which can cause disease; and gobble up flies, which can ruin a picnic. Additionally, spiders are an important food source for many other species.

## NATURAL HISTORY RECAP

**What do we know about spiders?** Spiders belong to the largest group of animals on Earth—the arthropods. The name means "jointed foot," and all members of this group have tough exoskeletons, lack a backbone, and fill almost every possible habitat on the planet. Different from insects and other invertebrates, spiders belong to the group known as arachnids, which they share with ticks, mites, and scorpions. More specifically, the roughly 45,000 species of spiders belong to a subgroup all their own (called an order), known as Araneae. With a body divided into two main sections, the cephalothorax in the front and the abdomen in the back, spiders lack antennae, but all possess the ability to produce silk. The use of silk that is most familiar to people is the production of the web, but only about half the spiders in the world use a web to catch prey. The silk is also used by some species to make shelter, move from one location to another, or attract a mate, among other functions.

Just about every species of spider is a predator. Though many eat other invertebrates, some will catch small vertebrates as well, including lizards, frogs, rodents, and birds. A close-up image of a spider reveals its predatory adaptations. The chelicerae function as a spider's jaws, which are tipped with the fangs. The pedipalps are typically longer appendages that are used to sense a spider's surrounding by touch. Though they look like legs, they are not counted as such (spiders have four pairs of walking legs). Additional information about a spider's environment is provided by the hairs that cover the body and legs. Spiders can use these specialized structures to "hear" their surroundings as vibrations. Like the number of their walking legs, many spiders have eight eyes, though some species have fewer. Despite having multiple eyes, many spiders have poor eyesight, instead relying on touch, vibration, and taste to explore their surroundings.

A flower crab spider waits for prey.

**Why are they in danger?** In our homes, where arachnids are seldom welcomed, spiders can be harmed by pesticides and other chemicals, and often webs are destroyed as we tidy things up. The same threat persists outdoors as well, with pesticides killing prey and harming the spiders directly. As with many species in the wild, the most harmful threat is habitat loss—the clearing of forest, meadows, and other natural places where spiders thrive. Additional problems arise due to climate change and the pet trade (there are a surprising number of people who like to keep spiders as pets). Of the thousands of spider species around the world, only a very small number are being studied in enough detail to understand threats and the status of their population.

**How can we help?** Not only can we conduct surveys to find out what species inhabit our gardens, parks, and other habitats, but we can also spread the word about the importance of spiders and how very fascinating they are!

## SEARCHING FOR SPIDERS

### LESSON OVERVIEW

In the words of Hagrid from the Harry Potter series, "Seriously misunderstood creatures, spiders are." It is likely that their appearance, their habits, and the fact that they often occupy places we do not like to go perpetuate the fear of spiders. However, spiders are essential predators of other invertebrates, are found in some of the most beautiful habitats on the planet, and are really cool creatures to observe.

In this activity you are presented with invertebrate data that came from two of our park studies. We sampled a local meadow by using sweep nets and pitfall traps. All the organisms that were caught are included in the data tables shown here. Each group and the number of individuals from that group are presented in the tables.

### LEARNING OBJECTIVES

1. Determine the diversity of spiders in a meadow habitat from two different sampling efforts.
2. Establish why different sampling efforts may result in different diversity results.
3. Compare the presence of spiders in a meadow with the presence of other invertebrates.
4. Describe the important roles of spiders in meadow ecosystems.
5. Make a pie graph to show the breakdown of invertebrate diversity data from the meadow samples collected with the two different methods.

Pitfall traps waiting to be examined

Community science in the field with a sweep net

Sweep net

## TASKS

1. Using the table to the right, calculate the percentage of the invertebrates collected in each sample (sweep net and pitfall trap) that were spiders.
2. Make a pie graph to display the percentage of each invertebrate group present. The groups should include:

   spiders
   beetles
   flies
   butterflies and moths
   ants, bees, and wasps
   true bugs
   grasshoppers and crickets
   damselflies and dragonflies

Complete this task both for sweep net data and pitfall trap data.

3. Identify which of the other invertebrate groups are eaten by spiders.
4. Why are both sampling methods, net sweeping and pitfall traps, needed to collect spiders?
5. What would happen if the abundance of spiders was to decline in the meadow? Consider their role as predators.
6. Other than spiders being important predators, can you name and describe another important role that they play in meadows and other habitats?

## SPIDERS IN THE MEADOW COMMUNITY

| Sweep Net | Pitfall Trap |
|---|---|
| katydid | field cricket |
| ten-spot dragonfly | gnat |
| micrathena spider | bark crab spider |
| monarch caterpillar | ground beetle |
| milkweed bug | carpenter ant |
| American copper butterfly | ghost spider |
| robber fly | zebra jumping spider |
| May beetle | green stink bug |
| honeybee | weevil |
| tree cricket | black ant |
| banded garden spider | leafhopper |
| treehopper | wolf spider |
| goldenrod crab spider | grass spider |
| cabbage white butterfly | click beetle |
| green darner | woolly bear caterpillar |
| bottle fly | trapdoor spider |
| mosquito | aphid |
| red-legged grasshopper | |
| spotted orbweaver spider | |
| sweat bee | |
| yellow sac spider | |
| potato beetle | |
| Japanese beetle | |
| two-striped grasshopper | |
| painted lady butterfly | |
| bold jumping spider | |
| bumblebee | |
| black-and-yellow garden spider | |
| spittlebug | |
| ladybird beetle | |

# INVESTIGATION 2

## ADVENTURES WITH ARACHNIDS

### LESSON OVERVIEW

Our homes and gardens support more wildlife than most people would expect. Sometimes we are unnerved by the presence of a leggy roommate—insects, spiders, and other invertebrates often find exactly what they need under the roof they share with you! In the case of spiders, we should learn more about the benefits they provide to us by their predatory nature.

In this activity you will match the spider species that can be found in or around your home with the pest species that they are likely to encounter in their home habitat.

### LEARNING OBJECTIVES

1. Describe the habitats of different spider species.
2. Match spider species with likely prey species from habitat descriptions.
3. Describe the ecosystem services provided by spiders.
4. Establish the importance of spiders in human environments.

### PART 1: SPECIES DESCRIPTION TASKS

1. Provide a general description of the behavior, habitat, and location around the home or garden of the following spider species:

wolf spider
zebra jumping spider
barn spider
yellow garden spider
common house spider
goldenrod crab spider

2. Various insect species can be considered pests in and around the home. The following is a list of some of these species:

termites
ants
mosquitoes
housefly
camel crickets
aphids

Describe the potential problems for humans brought about by each of these insect species in the Spider Prey Diagram.

### PART 2: PREDATOR/PREY MATCH TASKS

3. Label the spiders and the insects below from the lists in Part 1.
4. Match the species of insect with the spider that could potentially keep their abundance in check. All spider species should be matched with a single insect (some of these spiders could likely come across more than one species of insect).

# SPIDER PREY DIAGRAM

# APPENDIX 1

## COMMUNITY SCIENCE DATA SHEET

**PROJECT NAME:**

**DESCRIPTION:**

**LOCATION:**

**TIME:**

**WEATHER:**

**PARTNER/S:**

**DATA/CALCULATIONS:**

**NOTES / SKETCHES:**

# APPENDIX 2

## ANSWER KEY TO INVESTIGATIONS

### "HORSESHOE CRAB RESCUE" INVESTIGATION 1

1. 45 total horseshoe crabs stranded; 1 of every 9 crabs is female (11% female), 8 of every 9 crabs are male (89% male).
2. The ratio of male-to-female is much different from spawning horseshoe crabs on the beach. The maximum ratio is typically 5:1, and the ratio of crabs trapped in rubble is 8:1.
3. When they emerge to spawn, larger females typically dig down into the sand to deposit their eggs. Males typically stay at the surface. This may leave them more prone to being washed into rubble or other structures. The larger females are also heavier. This may reduce the number washed into rubble as well.
4. Survival of trapped crabs is based on exposure to drying out. Horseshoe crabs that are trapped under structures away from the drying effects of the sun and elevated temperature may survive longer. In addition, horseshoe crabs trapped between high tide and low tide sea levels will be covered by the water twice a day, which likely allows them to survive for longer periods of time. Horseshoe crabs trapped in structures that expose them to predators such as gulls will have an impact on survival. Some structures may physically crush the crabs, which can cause them to die.

### "HORSESHOE CRAB RESCUE" INVESTIGATION 2

1. Length of each beach:
   Lighthouse Beach (*top left*) = 700 meters
   Pleasant Beach (*lower left*) = 500 meters

**RESOURCES:**

Links for Tutorials on Building Graphs in Google Sheets
https://www.youtube.com/watch?v=dwjCRddlxEI
https://www.youtube.com/watch?v=SeNtoBld8vY
https://www.youtube.com/watch?v=nAsS3PeQ92E

   Long Beach (*center*) = 1,300 meters (1.3 km)
   Fishing Beach (*right*) = 900 meters
2. Percentages of beach makeup:
   Lighthouse Beach = 14% mud, 29% vegetation, 57% sand
   Pleasant Beach = 20% vegetation, 80% sand
   Long Beach = 15% vegetation, 38% seawall, 46% sand
   Fishing Beach = 56% rock/rubble, 33% sand, 11% mud
3. Percentage of horseshoe crabs trapped or flipped:
   Lighthouse Beach = 67% flipped, 33% trapped
   Pleasant Beach = 91% flipped, 9% trapped
   Long Beach = 59% flipped, 41% trapped
   Fishing Beach = 28% flipped, 72% trapped
4. Pleasant Beach, although the shortest beach, offers the best natural habitat for spawning (sand). The percentage of horseshoe crabs flipped is greatest on this beach, which suggests only natural events are associated with crabs needing rescue.
5. Fishing Beach shows the greatest percentage of trapped horseshoe crabs (72%) and the greatest overall percentage of human features that could trap horseshoe crabs (56% rock/rubble).

## "NIGHT LIGHTS" INVESTIGATION 1

**1.** Mean (average) # flashes:
Data set 1 = 137
Data set 2 = 89
Data set 3 = 23
Data set 4 = 6

**2.**

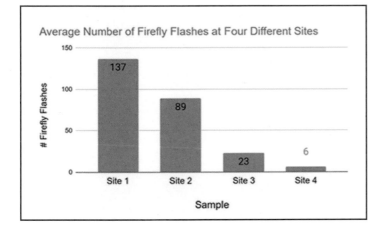

**3.** Researchers found that less light will likely result in more firefly flashes, and more light will likely result in fewer flashes. This includes the immediate study site and adjacent sites. Light presence tends to reduce the activity of fireflies.

**4.** Too much light, resulting in fewer flashes, could reduce communication between individuals, which can limit mating and, for some species, finding food (attracting others so they can be captured).

**5.** Answers could include bats, moths, opossums, owls, flying squirrels. Depending on the species, the effects may include finding food, avoiding becoming food, navigation, mating, and competition with other species.

**6.** Set up an experiment that will compare the effects of "typical" lights with red lights. The study sites should have similar backyard habitats (similar size and resources for fireflies or other species). Ideally, find several sites so that you can collect data from more than one site per light type and calculate the average. Determine what you will monitor as part of your study (number of flashes of fireflies, diversity of moths, number of visits by nocturnal mammals, etc.). Collect data several times during the study (perhaps every other night for a month). Be sure to collect data on weather and other factors that could also have an impact on the species and activities you are studying.

## "NIGHT LIGHTS" INVESTIGATION 2

Garden designs should emphasize natural features—meadow/wildflower vegetation, trees, shrubs, and leaf litter. Distribution of habitat for fireflies and their prey should also reveal availability at multiple sites throughout the garden. Knowledge of adjacent properties to the garden would help guide placement of features (use of pesticides by neighbors, presence of lights or other adverse conditions, or features that could harm fireflies).

Designs will vary, and an important part of this activity is to emphasize student description and discussion of designs. Additional research on firefly needs will allow students to enhance their garden layouts.

## "FINDING FROGS" INVESTIGATION 1

**1–11.** Follow prompts on the USGS Frog Quiz website (https://www.pwrc.usgs.gov/frogquiz).

Here is a sample of what a finished field guide might look like, based on the Pine Barrens region of New Jersey.
**List of species from the Pine Barrens of New Jersey in June include:**
Pine Barrens tree frog, gray treefrog, Fowler's toad, southern leopard frog, carpenter frog, green frog
**Habitat for species from sample inventory:**
*Pine Barrens tree frog*—Acidic waters of swamps and bogs, intermittent pools during breeding, and pine forests during nonbreeding season
*gray treefrog*—Swamps, ponds, and intermittent pools during breeding season, and forests during nonbreeding season
*Fowler's toad*—Ponds, intermittent pools, and shallow lake margins during breeding season, and sandy, vegetated, open habitat during nonbreeding season.
*southern leopard frog*—Shallow freshwater habitats during breeding season, and wet, grassy habitats near water during the nonbreeding season
*carpenter frog*—Sphagnum wetlands and bogs during the breeding and nonbreeding seasons
*green frog*—During breeding and nonbreeding seasons, found near any body of freshwater
**Call descriptions** can be anything from chirps, clucks, clicks, quonks, etc.—students must listen to frog calls to describe. It will be fun to compare how different groups describe frog calls for the same species.

## Conservation status for species from sample inventory:

*Pine Barrens tree frog*—Threatened in New Jersey, limited to Pine Barrens of New Jersey

*gray tree frog (southern subspecies)*—Endangered in New Jersey, found only in high-quality habitat in southern counties of New Jersey. Northern subspecies population abundant and secure throughout the state.

*Fowler's toad*—Found in suitable habitat throughout the state of New Jersey

*southern leopard frog*—Found in suitable habitat throughout the state of New Jersey

*carpenter frog*—Found mostly in suitable acidic habitat throughout the southern part of New Jersey

*green frog*—Found in suitable, and sometimes human-impacted, freshwater habitats throughout the entire state of New Jersey

## Priority Ranking for species from sample inventory:

The following ranking (from highest priority to lowest) is based on official conservation statues, distribution throughout the state, and habitats required to support breeding and nonbreeding populations:

Pine Barrens tree frog—highest priority
gray tree frog (southern subspecies)
carpenter frog
Fowler's toad
southern leopard frog
green frog—lowest priority

2. Maximum species breeding—only the last week of May shows all species potentially breeding (shown in green). To include the greatest diversity of frogs and toads in a study, this would be the only week to conduct a study.

3. Maximum species tadpole presence—all of June and early July are likely to show tadpole activity for all species (shown in blue). In terms of selecting a study week for tadpoles, it seems reasonable that the middle of June would be best; in case development of some species runs late or early, the third week of June is right in the middle of maximum species tadpole development.

4. See comments above.

5. Additional study recommendations:

Consider different habitats (streams, ponds, lakes, swamps, etc.)—which species breed in each habitat type?

Compare breeding activity and tadpole presence with next year's study. For example, if a species does not breed at a given site for a given year, will it be present next year?

Using calls or visual sightings, which species were most dominant at a given site?

What human pressures are near sites that may not have species that should be present given a specific time of year?

## "FINDING FROGS" INVESTIGATION 2

1. Sample spreadsheet

| Species Breeding | MARCH WK 1 | WK 2 | WK 3 | WK 4 | APRIL WK 1 | WK 2 | WK 3 | WK 4 | MAY WK 1 | WK 2 | WK 3 | WK 4 | JUNE WK 1 | WK 2 | WK 3 | WK 4 | JULY WK 1 | WK 2 | WK 3 | WK 4 | AUGUST WK 1 | WK 2 | WK 3 | WK 4 |
|---|---|---|---|---|---|---|---|---|---|---|---|---|---|---|---|---|---|---|---|---|---|---|---|---|
| American Bullfrog | O | O | O | O | O | O | O | O | O | O | O | XO | XO | XO | XO | XO | XO | XO | XO | XO | O | O | O | O |
| American Toad | | | | | X | XO | XO | XO | XO | XO | XO | XO | XO | XO | XO | XO | XO | XO | XO | XO | XO | XO | O | O |
| E. Spadefoot Toad | | | | | X | XO | XO | XO | XO | XO | XO | XO | XO | O | O | O | O | O | | | | | | |
| Fowler's Toad | | | | | | | | | | | | X | XO | XO | XO | XO | XO | XO | XO | XO | XO | XO | O | O |
| Gray Tree Frog | | | | | | | | | | | | X | XO | XO | XO | XO | XO | XO | XO | XO | O | O | O | O |
| Green Frog | O | O | O | O | XO | XO | XO | XO | XO | XO | XO | XO | XO | XO | XO | XO | XO | XO | XO | XO | XO | XO | XO | XO |
| N. Leopard Frog | XO | XO | XO | XO | XO | XO | XO | XO | XO | XO | XO | XO | O | O | O | O | O | O | O | O | O | O | O | O |
| Pickerel Frog | X | XO | XO | XO | XO | XO | XO | XO | XO | XO | XO | XO | XO | O | O | O | O | O | O | O | O | O | O | O |
| Spring Peeper | X | XO | XO | XO | XO | XO | XO | XO | XO | XO | XO | XO | XO | XO | XO | XO | O | O | O | O | O | O | O | O |
| Wood Frog | X | XO | XO | XO | XO | XO | XO | XO | XO | XO | XO | XO | XO | XO | XO | XO | XO | XO | XO | XO | O | O | O | O |

| previous breeding season's tadpoles | peak breeding diversity | peak tadpole activity |
|---|---|---|

x - breeding occuring
o - tadpoles present

## "MYSTERY MUSSEL" INVESTIGATION 1

**1.** A) Agriculture—Fertilizers can increase algae in the water which can disrupt food webs, grow over the surface of ponds, or both. Pesticides can be toxic to mussels and fish (species that mussels require for reproduction). Elevated sediment can cover habitat and even the mussels themselves and may also hinder filter feeding.
B) Dams—Dams disrupt water flow and alter habitat—upstream and downstream, blocking fish movement (some species are needed by mussels for reproduction).
C) Invasive species—Invasive species may eat mussels and/or compete with them for habitat and food.
D) Climate change—Extreme precipitation events can flood streams and rivers, altering habitat or even washing mussels away. Prolonged droughts can result in dropping water levels, potentially exposing mussels to drying out. Extreme temperatures can stress mussel species adapted to cooler water.

**2.** Mussel threats:
Agriculture—Sediment, fertilizers, and pesticides can cause pollution in streams and rivers that can be toxic to mussels, affect food availability, and alter habitat.
Residential—Sediment, fertilizers, and trash can foul waterways. Salt runoff from road treatment in the winter can pollute streams and rivers. Human use of the water can alter habitat. For example, fishing line and hooks, boating, and wading can alter bottom habitat. Collection of mussels can reduce populations.
Urban—Various pollutants as described above can enter waterways. Paving, channeling (altering the course of streams/rivers), dams, and increased flooding from impervious surfaces (water that cannot enter the ground will run off into surface water and quickly change flow and water levels).
Forest—Tree roots stabilize the soil and reduce erosion of sediment. Vegetation will absorb excess nutrients and reduce the energy of runoff. Natural surfaces will absorb water into the ground, reducing the incidence of flooding. Trees shade the surface water and keep the water temperature from getting too warm in summer, which can stress mussel species.

**3.** Matches for communities and sample locations:
Study site A will have the least mussel richness (number of species), only one species, since the varied effects of urban landscapes will limit diversity.
Study site B will have the second greatest diversity of mussels (five species)—since, though agricultural runoff may affect the waterway, much of the landscape is forested and thus offers good habitat and support for mussel species.
Study site C will have the sample with two mussel species. The landscape is residential and agricultural surrounding this location. As such, impacts will be potentially significant, as described above.
Study site D will have the greatest overall mussel diversity (eight species). Completely surrounded by forest cover, this natural setting will support maximum mussel diversity,

since the ecology and habitat of this stream section will be healthy. All benefits that come from a natural land cover will benefit the mussel community.

**4.** It is likely that all groups will arrive at the same results, provided that the description of potential impacts from the various land cover types was thorough.

## "MYSTERY MUSSEL" INVESTIGATION 2

Based on description, habitat, and size, the identifications of the mystery mussels are as follows:

mystery mussel 1—green floater
mystery mussel 2—eastern elliptio
mystery mussel 3—eastern pond mussel
mystery mussel 4—yellow lamp mussel

*Note: Habitat and measurements from the page should match the description and range for the identifications summarized above.*

## "THE LANTERNFLY HAS LANDED" INVESTIGATION 1

**1.** 20 trees total in each block
**2.** 131 in block 1, 140 in block 2
**3.** Total lanternflies for each tree species:

| Block 1 | # trees | total lanternflies |
|---|---|---|
| sugar maple | 3 | 18 |
| silver linden | 1 | 1 |
| red maple | 5 | 91 |
| sweet gum | 2 | 1 |
| tulip poplar | 2 | 4 |
| black walnut | 1 | 4 |
| sycamore | 3 | 10 |
| northern red oak | 2 | 1 |
| Callery pear | 1 | 1 |

| Block 2 | # trees | total lanternflies |
|---|---|---|
| sugar maple | 2 | 16 |
| silver linden | 2 | 8 |
| red maple | 4 | 89 |
| sweet gum | 1 | 2 |
| tulip poplar | 2 | 3 |
| black cherry | 2 | 5 |
| sycamore | 2 | 9 |
| northern red oak | 3 | 4 |
| black walnut | 1 | 3 |
| mulberry | 1 | 1 |

**4.**

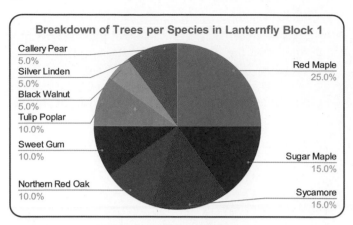

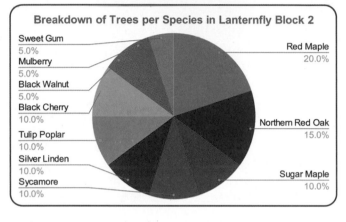

**5.**

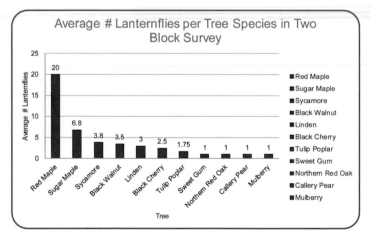

**6.** Overall tree diversity (number of different tree species) is similar between the two blocks. There were tree species found in only one block or the other, but their abundance was limited to one individual, and the average number of lanternflies found on these species was low.

Maples, followed by sycamore, hosted the greatest average number of lanternflies, and these tree species were present in similar number when comparing the two blocks. Thus, it is not surprising to find similar numbers of lanternflies on the trees in block 1 when compared with block 2.

**7.** Regarding new tree plantings in town, in terms of lanternfly data, it would be recommended to stay away from maples and sycamore. A focus on native species could emphasize any of the other species (Callery pear is not native so should not be emphasized). The town should consider a combination of the remaining species so as to maximize habitat and aesthetic appeal for the community.

## "THE LANTERNFLY HAS LANDED" INVESTIGATION 2

**1–2.** Infestation rates:

*2019*—total max. distance spread from epicenter = 180 mi., about 300 km; direction: W, SW, and NE
Five states—VA, PA, DE, MD, NJ

*2020*—total max. distance spread from epicenter = 195 mi., about 325 km; direction: W and E
Six states—VA, PA, DE, MD, NJ, WV

*2021*—total max. distance spread from epicenter = 300 mi., about 500 km; direction: W, NW, E, SE, SW
Nine states—VA, PA, DE, MD, NJ, WV, OH, NY, CT

*2022*—total max. distance spread from epicenter = 555 mi., about 925 km; direction: SW, NE, NW and N
Eleven states—VA, PA, DE, MD, NJ, WV, OH, NY, CT, MA, IN

*2023 (projection)*—states to include VT, NC, and RI—very close to existing infestation zones and have ecosystems and habitats that will likely support lanternflies.

**3.** The distribution of lanternflies is likely not contiguous, because lanternflies can spread by people (vehicles) and by products (wood, landscaping materials). As such, they can be moved considerable distances over short periods of time. In addition, development and human activities may also break up the preferred habitat for lanternflies. Thus, they may be present but not have ideal enough habitat to cause infestation in certain areas.

**4.** Campaigns to educate people about the accidental movement of lanternflies can help limit distribution. Community and agricultural campaigns can be established to monitor and capture lanternflies in regions where they are already present. Traps can be set for their capture (care must be taken to avoid harming beneficial insects and other species). Habitat can be enhanced to increase natural predators of lanternflies. In the winter, egg masses can be identified and removed before hatching in the spring.

## "THE GREAT SHOREBIRD MIGRATION" INVESTIGATION 1

Diet and feeding strategies for shorebird species represented in this investigation can be explored using the Cornell University All About Birds website: https://www.allaboutbirds.org/news/.

1. On page 46, *top*: whimbrel; *bottom*: short-billed dowitcher. On page 47, *top, from left to right*: red knot, ruddy turnstone, sanderling, and piping plover; *bottom*: American oystercatcher. The seven shorebird species differ in their overall body size, bill length and shape, leg length, and feeding behavior.

2. The features described above allow these birds to feed close to other species that may eat similar things. Longer legs may allow birds to wade a bit deeper in the water. The behavior of moving back and forth at the wave's edge allows them to pick up food items exposed by the energy of the water. A strong, stiff bill allows a bird to pry open a mussel or oyster. The shape and length of a bill allow some shorebirds to pull prey from burrows.

3. Though some species may feed at different sites and on varied prey, a typical match sequence for the birds represented would be

   Food source A (crustaceans at wave edge) = sanderlings

   Food source B (worms in the sediment in shallow water) = short-billed dowitcher

   Food source C (small clams near the water's edge) = red knot

   Food source D (mussels and oysters) = American oystercatcher

   Food source E (invertebrates found in deep, curved burrows) = whimbrel

   Food source F (diverse invertebrates found on and under pilings) = ruddy turnstone

   Food source G (surface invertebrates in high-tide zone) = piping plover

*Note: Consider which birds are more specific to one food source and which could eat various prey items and in various locations (specialist vs. generalists).*

## "THE GREAT SHOREBIRD MIGRATION" INVESTIGATION 2

1. Moving vehicles would likely be the most problematic human disturbance, since they can move fast and drivers may not notice birds nearby that can be flushed (caused to move away) or hit by drivers. Dogs (especially off leash) would likely be another major disturbance, since they can run quickly and may be prone to chase birds simply by instinctive behavior.
Ranking (most problematic to least):

   *Moving vehicle*—fast; may run over or scare away birds over a large area/distance

   *Dog*—fast; behavior may result in constant chasing of birds, preventing resting/feeding

   *Biker*—fast; biker may not notice birds

   *Jogger*—though not as fast as other disturbances, approach may be perceived as threat

   *Walker*—a human moving, even slowly, may be perceived as threat

   *Fisher*—may be perceived as threat; fishing line presents tangling threat

   *Parked vehicle*—large unnatural object may block habitat view

2. Effect of human activity by section:

   *Beach section 1*—seven types of disturbance (total = 48), eight moving vehicles. Only a single bird species present, totaling forty individuals.

   *Beach section 2*—seven types of disturbance (total = 36), six moving vehicles, three shorebird species present, totaling sixty individuals

   *Beach section 3*—five types of disturbance (total = 20), four moving vehicles, three shorebird species present, totaling eighty-one individuals

*Note: Remaining two beach sections are beyond a barrier that prevents vehicles from entering.*

   *Beach section 4*—three types of disturbance (nine total), no moving vehicles, five shorebird species present, totaling 173 individuals

   *Beach section 5*—one type of disturbance (three total), no moving vehicles, seven shorebird species present, totaling 480 individuals

3. Red knots, short-billed dowitchers, and whimbrels are found only in the last two sections, suggesting that they may be less tolerant to human disturbances.

   Where more moving vehicles and dogs are present, there are fewer species and individuals (supports ranking above).

   Bird richness (number of different species) and abundance increase as total disturbances decline.

   Sanderlings are found in every beach section, suggesting they may be more tolerant of human disturbance.

   The last two sections show a dramatic increase in number of species and number of individuals, suggesting that keeping vehicles out (and likely dogs as well) will offer better feeding and resting habitat for shorebirds.

*Note: You may identify additional key connections from the data.*

## "SOS—SAVE OUR SPIDERS" INVESTIGATION 1

**1. Percentage of spider for each sample:**
In the pitfall traps, 6/17 invertebrates were spiders = 35%.
In the sweep nets, 7/30 invertebrates were spiders = 23%.

**2a. Pitfall traps:**
- 6 spider species
- 3 beetle species
- 1 fly species
- 1 butterfly and moth species
- 2 ant, bee, and wasp species
- 3 true bug species
- 1 grasshopper and cricket species
- 0 damselfly and dragonfly species

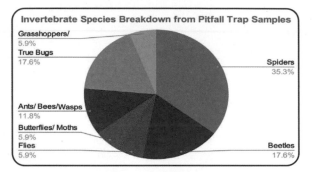

**2b. Sweep nets:**
- 7 spider species
- 4 beetle species
- 3 fly species
- 4 butterfly and moth species
- 3 ant, bee, and wasp species
- 3 true bug species
- 4 grasshopper and cricket species
- 2 damselfly and dragonfly species

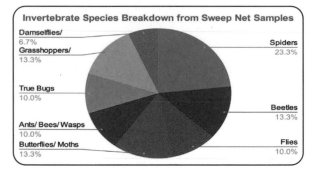

3. All invertebrate species found in pitfall trap and sweep net samples are eaten by spiders.
4. Using both methods ensures that spider diversity will be represented from a variety of habitats: ground, leaf litter, grass, meadow, shrubs.
5. The food web would be out of balance. Spiders are important predators that, as a community, keep the populations of other insects and invertebrates in check. If the populations of prey species were to increase, other connections in the ecosystems would be harmed; for example, overbrowsing by leaf eaters, or an increase in invasive insects that could outcompete native species.
6. Spiders feed other species, such as birds, amphibians, reptiles, and mammals. Additionally, the silk that spiders create is used by a variety of birds for nest material.

## "SOS—SAVE OUR SPIDERS" INVESTIGATION 2

1. Spider species descriptions:
   *wolf spider*—Large, agile spider with good eyesight; excellent hunters. Occupy a diversity of habitats and can be found in basements and gardens around and in the home.
   *yellow garden spider*—Web-building spider often found in gardens and meadows, but also under eaves of homes and on the exterior of outbuildings.
   *zebra jumping spider*—Found commonly associated with human habitations, fences, walls, and surfaces indoors, they are agile predators.
   *common house spider*—Web-building spiders that often occupy out-of-the-way spaces in homes, such as attics, corners. and basements
   *barn spider*—Often building their webs near wooden structures, they commonly occupy spaces around outdoor lighting, since this may attract insects that are common prey at night.
   *goldenrod crab spider*—Commonly hunting on goldenrod, milkweed, and other flower species. They may adapt to the color of the flower species they occupy, though they will blend best to white and yellow backgrounds. With good vision, they often hunt during the day.
2. Potential problems for humans per spider prey species:
   *aphids*—Sapsuckers that when abundant can damage plants in the garden
   *housefly*—Can be a nuisance in the home or garden and can transmit disease
   *ants*—Considered a nuisance in the kitchen or pantry since they can get into food
   *mosquito*—Nuisance species, largely outside the home; can cause various diseases
   *camel cricket*—Will dine on fabric, cardboard, and fruit and can be damaging to stored items and furniture fabrics, often in basements
   *termites*—Can cause allergic reactions when abundant and can damage wood structures in a home
3. Spiders from left to right: wolf spider, yellow garden spider, barn spider, goldenrod crab spider, common house spider, zebra jumping spider
Insects from left to right: aphid, termite, mosquito, camel cricket, ant, fly
4. There may be various combinations of predator/prey matches for our six spider species and six insect pests. With the goal to use each spider once, the following matches are referenced:
wolf spider—camel cricket
barn spider—mosquito
goldenrod crab spider—ant
common house spider—housefly
zebra jumping spider—termite
yellow garden spider—aphid